At Arm's Length

poems

Isabella J Mansfield

Publisher, Editor, and Cover Art:
Isabella J Mansfield

Author Photo:
Ryan Rupprecht

Press, Author Inquires, and Booking:
isabellajmansfield@gmail.com

Printed in the USA

poems

A Note From Isabella

Five Star binders really had a hold on me as a 90's kid. Yes, I know they're still around. I also know the Trapper Keeper will *always* be superior to a zippered Five Star, but my black, zippered binder offered a secure place for loose notebook paper, sticky notes, scraps, receipts, and a few paper napkins, covered in poems.

Poetry offered solace for me as I learned to balance being Regular Teen Girl with Newly Disabled Girl. I had standard teen girl drama: wanting to dress cool and appear cool and impress god knows who, a developing body, acne, homework. Then there was the bonus content: learning to live with and around a wheelchair, a body that is now not functioning below the waist, hospital visits, physical therapy, and so much more. I never wrote about my disability, sticking to teen girl topics like boys and broken hearts, teen angst and sadness. Before I reached high school, the collection outgrew a pocket folder and graduated to the Five Star zippered. It was covered in stickers and messages written with White-Out pens. When I moved out of my mother's home at 19, I packed it tenderly in a box with photo albums and other important memories.

In 2014, I found Five Star in a box in the closet. I flipped through each soft page, squinting to read the faded graphite, and typed each one into Google Docs. The idea to self publish was obviously absurd, but I thought about the evenings I spent at The Coffee Bean, holding Five Star to my chest, waiting my turn to share for Poetry Night. The youngest by at least 30 years, surrounded by these experienced, adult poets, with their own binders and more impressive still—some reading from published books. HARDCOVER books, even. She could never. Could she? On December 8th, 2014, I clicked a button and At Arm's Length was published, and available for purchase. Of course, this wasn't going to become a *thing*. Just putting it out there "for posterity's sake."

Ten years later. It's 2024, and I sit here with a document titled "At Arm's Length 10th Anniversary Ideas" and I gotta tell you: they're all terrible. I wanted to do something special and impressive for the 10th anniversary, but every idea was met with struggle, and more than a little embarrassment at the work I'd published. How do you look back at your younger self, your earlier art, when you know how far you've come and how much you've learned? It has taken me months to realize: you don't. You don't have to impress anyone, just like you didn't have to impress The Cool Girls in middle school, or the Adult Poets in the coffee shop. Growth is vital in our lives. I am not a teenager scribbling poems in the margins of her homework (ok fine. writing poems *instead* of doing homework.) I am not a new mom in 2014, putting the work out there "just because." I am living a dream I never knew I had, and it is beautiful, just the way it is.

And so, friend, in these pages I present At Arm's Length as it was originally published. Minimal editing. No black out poems or notes like "yikes. this sucks." (actual idea I'd considered.) No hiding the very real emotions of a 17 year old on the brink of adulthood. Yes, it still makes me cringe to read, like an old yearbook or diary, and while I will secretly hope nobody judges this book too harshly, I am still proud that it exists.

- Isabella

How To Write Poetry Books

I don't know what the hell
I am doing.

I don't expect anyone to read this
especially not you.

Some things are better left
unsaid

some, better left
unwritten

These are not
those things.

Heat Lightning

somewhere,
someone is clinging
to a loved one,
afraid of thunder.
I hear nothing,
and am comforted
by the thought
of being alone.

I Wondered

I wondered what it was
about you that made me
nervous
but I let you kiss me
anyway
I closed my eyes
and let it all happen
now, you glance at me
only when you think
they can't see you

Change of Heart

There is a hole
in my favorite jeans.
You spoke, and I picked
at the fraying denim,
plucking tiny, blue threads
until the whole of my knee
was exposed; watching
everything unravel at my hand.

I sat on the floor
and let cool tears
fall from the eyes
you used to love. I couldn't
be bothered to wipe them away;
they made little, dark,
wet spots on my jeans,
and disappeared after you.

The Drive

I sipped a diet Coke
and slipped into
a daydream.
Dazed, I sat in traffic
in the first snow
of the season.
The flicker of
the dashboard clock
caught my eye,
ending the reverie.
I sat staring
at the snowfall:
watching my breath
curl and billow its way
through each tiny flake.
I thought about the
miles between us,
as well as the distance.

"You're Always Sick," He Said

"You never really get better.
You never really heal."

I wanted to tell him that
I'm sick from swallowing back
all the things I wanted to say to him.

but he's right;
I never really heal.

When You Speak

When you speak
I absorb the details,
I remember little utterances
and tones in your voice.
I replay nice things you've said
like a tape recorder.
Fast forwarding to the good parts,
rewinding, to hear them again.
Sometimes, I want to play it backwards
and find the hidden messages.

My Summer Job

I wish I had
a single brick
to hurl through
this window
just so I could hear
the glass shatter

I Could Scream

I could scream for hours.
I could scream until my throat
was raw.

It would make no difference
except you might yell at me
for bleeding.

November

Here it is now,
nearly November.

My mind wanders to
holiday things and
I can't help but wonder
where the year has gone.

I search for discarded
calendar pages—scrambling
as if to go back
to each lost opportunity

and before I know it
I've missed everything.

Devil's Night

Last night seems so far away.
Last night you seemed so far away.
I couldn't remember the last two days if I tried,
so I won't try.

This time of year, we all wear a mask;
mine to cover smeared makeup and tears.
Yours, handsome as always;
scarier than ever.

Discontentment

the tears just sat there,
distorting my view,
without falling,
for ages.

they felt cold
on my eyes,
stubbornly sitting,
refusing to fall or be
wiped away.

they blurred the edges
of everything
and made me wonder if
you'd really just said that
or if my ears were blurry, too.

such disdain, such disbelief
in your voice:
disheartening
dissuading
discouraging.

such a display,
these foolish tears,
sitting there
waiting to be
discovered

Spend Your Days

You spend your days
elsewhere
I spent my days
alone

I look forward to spending
my weekends with you
your weekends fill up
without me

You wonder what
the next thing is
I wonder when that
will be me

Lights Out

I don't turn the lights on
after the sun goes down.
There seems no point
in lighting an empty house.

When you're not here,
my day passes -
uneventful, it goes
without notice.

It gets late sometimes.
I go to bed alone;
the bed off balance
without you.

Your coming home
is sometimes worse
when I see you living
life without me.

In My Nightmares You Write Poems About Me

You wrote a poem for me
and gave it to me
written on the
back of a pink
neck tie
I was
flattered
until I
saw
the
noose
at
the end
and how
you strangled
my heart with it

"You Owe Me," He Said

my back to a corner
I am stuck
trapped

the missed opportunity
was yours, not mine
not now

exposed and feeling naked
you know
what I want

you
know
what

you
want
more

my weapons
and my guard down
you don't know

when
to
stop

He Still Makes Me Nervous

He still makes me nervous
just like when I was younger,
desperate to be wanted,

That stolen kiss in the dark,
the way he grazed my body
with his fingertips.

Hanging on every word
every breath, waiting
and waiting. and waiting.

Foolish

You have made
a fool of me.

foolish for believing
there was anything
behind your actions,
behind your wicked smile

I was young before -
too young and you knew it.
The clocks have changed,
calendar pages turned.

You resist it
I still feel naive,
and foolish as ever.

Sins and Transgressions

I want to burn the shirt I wore
when you touched me
and everything else
you were near

Let the acrid smell of
burning cotton
fill me up rather
than your bittersweet.

I can't forget the ways
I once wanted you
to touch me, still,
your invitation had expired

your welcome worn,
and I recoiled when
your skin brushed
my skin

In The Shadow, Down The Hall

the way you used to stare
I was so certain
I watched you
watching me,
certain there was
something
there is nothing there
you are hollow
empty
vacant
you say nothing
when you speak
words evaporating
without meaning
I was so certain
you were something
now I know
you were never there
at all

Hands

Your hands felt
different
than I was used to.
Smoother,
without fingerprints.
I expected they
would not leave
a mark on me;
but they did.

Your New Shoes

The way you held my hand
was not tender, was not kind,
but full of malice
and you would not
let me go.

I poured my heart out
but it spilled
and sloshed
and splashed
and made a mess of things.

You were so mad,
it had soiled your new shoes,
shiny and black.
The ones you bought
just to walk all over me.

Leave Me Wanting

you can't just
show up
then pretend
no time has passed
then pretend
nothing happened
you can't kiss me
then pretend
you didn't
then pretend
it meant nothing

The Audition

I've worked it all out.
I've played out this scene
so often in my head.
I know just where to stand
and what to say.
I'll tell you where
to place your hands,
how to move,
where to touch.
I'll play this part;
this borrowed confidence
this borrowed innocence.

Pantone Blues

Sometimes I wonder
if you're as bored as me.
Sometimes I think about
the last thing you said to me
the last time you kissed me,
the way it made me feel.
Sometimes I wonder
if you think about me
in the middle of your day, too.

San Antonio

You'd had a dream, and called
out out of the gray-blue sky,
to tell me all about it.
You never got so far
and teetered on the edge
of actual conversation.
I tottered back, wondering
what you wanted to tell me,
wondering what you wanted,
wondering if it was me.

Remembering the Alamo

It was raining
the day I left the city.
So strange to feel at home
a thousand miles from there.

I had not expected the call
or to feel so conflicted;
pulled one direction
drawn in another.

You weren't there with me
and I was no longer
certain of what I wanted.
You weren't there.

In the gray and haze,
the trees looked brighter
than I remembered
them to be.

By the Train Tracks, In Summer

We sat in my car, my back pressed
against the door, my legs across his lap.

I thought about the lies we told
to put us there that afternoon.

He could tell my mind was elsewhere
and tried to reel me back to him:

"The sun is in your eyes. They look different
in the sun, like warm caramel, a little bit red,"

Years later, he would tell me that was the day
he realized he was falling in love with me.

I felt sorry, knowing I had never
felt the same for him.

Haunted

In my dreams
you are more real
than you ever were.

In your dreams
you have nothing
to lose.

In your dreams
I have nowhere
to hide.

Things You Should Know

I never loved you
I dream about you

but I never loved you
You were only ever

a distraction.
I am weary from

resisting you
but I will keep trying

Tiny Pocket Tee

We all wore them then,
silly little shirts
that squeezed our curves,
bodies held close, held tight.

I had one with a tiny breast pocket
and I could feel your eyes
burning a hole into it
as you looked and looked.

When you finally spoke,
you asked what good it was,
such a tiny little thing, it barely fit
the fingertip you dared to slip inside it.

Tenth

when I kissed you
I closed my eyes,
afraid to open them
and discover
you had changed

Two Thousand Words

two thousand words
written in passion
or frustration

two thousand words
about loving you
or not loving you

two thousand words
to give me away
or keep you at arm's length

Isabella J Mansfield (she/her) writes about anxiety, intimacy, and body image both generally and as a woman with a disability. A three-time Pushcart Prize nominee, three-time Best of the Net Nominee and a Write Bloody McCarthy Prize Honorable Mention, Isabella is always looking for ways to bring a little humor into her deeply personal poems, and is almost never sorry to make you cry. She lives in Michigan with her husband and son.

Find her on Instagram and Facebook @isabellajmansfield

www.ingramcontent.com/pod-product-compliance
Lightning Source LLC
Chambersburg PA
CBHW070014100426
42741CB00012B/3240